MW00399418

ARIEL BOOKS

**Andrews McMeel
Publishing**
Kansas City

Abounding Wisdom

A SPIRITUAL TREASURY

EDITED, WITH COMMENTARY, BY

M. Scott Peck, M.D.

AUTHOR OF THE ROAD LESS TRAVELED

02 03 04 05 06 KWF 10 9 8 7 6 5 4 3 2 1

ISBN: 0-7407-2947-0

Library of Congress Catalog Card Number: 2002103792

Abounding
Wisdom

preface

In 2000, M. Scott Peck edited a collection of his favorite quotations in a beautiful volume called *Abounding Grace: An Anthology of Wisdom.* These words, gleaned from writers and thinkers, both famous and obscure, ancient and modern, were chosen to serve as guideposts on the road to a more spiritual existence.

Abounding Wisdom is developed from one of the twelve sections of *Abounding Grace.* The book not only includes all the quotations from the Wisdom section of *Abounding Grace* and Dr. Peck's introductory commentary, but a number of new quotations as well.

introduction

*T*HIS IS AN ANTHOLOGY of wisdom. To some indefinable extent, wisdom belongs in a class of its own: It subsumes all of the other virtues. Wisdom is the number one, the virtue par excellence, the one without equal.

That's a bold statement. "What about love?" you might well ask, and I would agree that it runs a close second. Still, it is second. Love indiscriminately, for instance, and you may well end up causing more harm than good. It is possible to be loving without being wise; it is not possible to be wise without loving.

Wisdom is a gift. Certain people seem to be almost born with an instinct for wisdom. On the other hand, I also believe that wisdom can be earned—that is to say, learned, but only by thinking about the challenges and experiences of our lives.

The majority seem to come down in favor of wisdom as earned, or at least as an "earned gift." Seek after wisdom, they advise; indeed, seek after it as nothing else, before anything else. Once again, I agree to a certain extent. Deep wisdom must be sought with all our strength. It must be chased down as if our whole life depended on it. But tell me this: What gives us the wisdom to choose to look for wisdom in the first place? From whence comes the burning desire to make wisdom our primary quest? It is hardly everyone's great goal, and no amount of admonition, such as these quotes, will likely change the fact.

Ultimately, I've come to believe that wisdom is more a gift than an earned character trait. I don't mean that it cannot be earned; to the contrary, it must be. I do mean, however, that the origin of the yearning to earn it is obscure and mysterious. Nevertheless, although the "science" of theology will never answer all the questions, I believe it has some big hints to offer.

In the late 1970s, a young woman, Marilyn Von Waldner, then a Catholic nun, composed and sang a collection of twelve Christian songs that were ultimately recorded and published under the title of What Return Can I Make?

(These songs were so personally powerful that they inspired me to write a book about them.) Two of the twelve songs are specifically about wisdom. The second begins with the resounding proclamation: "Wisdom is a spirit."

Although not spelled out in theological language, what Marilyn meant by being a spirit is that wisdom has its origin in "the Holy Spirit." That term (and its synonym, "the Holy Ghost") will sound like so much gibberish or mumbo jumbo to most nonbelievers. To most educated, devout Christians, however, its meaning is well defined: The Holy Spirit is the part of God that speaks to us directly. Sometimes this spirit— which I often think of as Sophia, after the goddess of wisdom—seems to speak to us through events or coincidences. Most dramatically She can speak to us through certain nighttime dreams (what Carl Jung referred to as "big dreams"). Most commonly She speaks to us through that "still, small voice"—a voice that would seem to come from within our own minds were it not for the fact that its words are far wiser than anything our own brains could cook up.

Space prevents me from recounting (as I have in some of my other, longer books) even a few of my personal encounters with the Holy Spirit, or attempting to explain my total faith in Her and my knowledge that Her gentle urging is the origin of wisdom. Let me simply state that the more I have wondered at the Holy Spirit the more I have been pushed to confront glory. Marilyn is also quite clear in her song that we need to actively seek the Holy Spirit, that we are not mere passive partners in the dance. Later in her song, however, she exalts in the fact that if you yearn and seek after the Holy Spirit in your life, then "the Lord will give you His mind." I know of no sentence in all of literature that so directly speaks to the human potential for glory. Actively seek wisdom from its font, the Holy Spirit, and it will upon occasion actually be possible for you to think with the mind of God!

This still begs the question of why or how it is that most do not attempt to thoroughly ally themselves with the mind of God, of why they have either never heard the voice of the Holy Spirit or recognized it as such. I would like to suggest that this might be because they deliberately "leave the phone off the hook." Yet why, again? St. Paul has said, "It is a terrifying thing to fall into the hands of the living God," alluding to the loss (or sense of loss) of control involved. To approach the same issue from a slightly different angle, I'd like to suggest that it is within our power or human strength to decide the kind of God we are going to believe in.

This is a radical thing to suggest . . . almost deviant. Our traditional notion is that God is all-powerful; that, whether we like it or not, we are His to mold; that God is what He is, and that although we may reject Him, it is certainly not in our puny, mortal human power to fashion Him. But I am not so sure about this. We may not be able to change the nature of God to suit our fancy, but I can tell you for sure that a change in our understanding of the nature of God will change us, change those around us, and hence change the world, no matter how minusculely.

I have said that God speaks to us through His or Her Holy Spirit in order to offer us wisdom. If we believe this, we are much less likely to leave the phone off the hook. But if we believe God does not speak to us, there's no point in even having that kind of phone or thinking that whatever wisdom we might possess is anything other than our own.

What kind of God do we want? One who speaks to us? One who is forever aloof? Or one who doesn't exist at all? Certain things, among them good or bad childhood experiences, may influence this choice, but never totally determine it. Whether we care for the responsibility or not, the choice is still ours.

Many questions remain, and I have only little hints. If there is a God . . . and if She does communicate with us . . . why should She be so interested in helping us toward wisdom?

In the long run I have nothing new to say. I never have had. Just a few new ways of saying it. I thought it would be nice to end this introduction with something about wisdom that was profoundly new and profoundly my own. But that was not the way the Holy Spirit chose to work. Instead, my inspiration has been corny and provincial.

There is a current, relatively recent weekly TV program entitled Touched by an Angel. Each episode centers around one or more people who are deeply troubled and a whole slew of angels God has sent to give them wisdom—a wisdom they generally don't want. Toward the end of each episode one of the angels (who looks as human as the rest of us) counters the character's resistance to the wisdom they offer by flatly stating: "I am an angel, sent to you by God because God wants you to know that He loves you." Through this they teach the character how important he or she is.

I could go on and on and on about wisdom. The subject excites me as no other. But in the end the most significant thing I have to point you in the path toward wisdom is to tell you that "God wants you to know that He loves you."

wisdom

*W*isdom is not to be obtained from textbooks, but must be coined out of human experience in the flame of life.

——Morris Raphael Cohen

I don't think much of a man who is not wiser today than he was yesterday.

——Abraham Lincoln

*E*very man is a damn fool for at least five minutes
every day. Wisdom consists in not exceeding
the limit.

—ELBERT HUBBARD

I do not believe that sheer suffering teaches. If
suffering alone taught, all the world would be
wise, since everyone suffers. To suffering must
be added mourning, understanding, patience,
love, openness, and the willingness to remain
vulnerable.

—ANNE MORROW LINDBERGH

*M*en who love wisdom should acquaint themselves with a great many particulars.
—HERACLITUS

*W*isdom consists not so much in knowing what to do in the ultimate as in knowing what to do next.
—HERBERT HOOVER

*M*any persons are both wise and handsome— but they would probably be still wiser were they less handsome.
—TALMUD

*I*t is easier to be wise on behalf of others than to
be so for ourselves.

—LA ROCHEFOUCAULD

*W*isdom never lies.

—HOMER

*Y*outh is the time to study wisdom; old age is the
time to practice it.

—JEAN-JACQUES ROUSSEAU

Through wisdom a house is built and through
understanding it is established.
—PROVERBS 24:3

Who is wise? He that learns from everyone.
—BENJAMIN FRANKLIN

The fool doth think he is wise, but the wise man
knows himself to be a fool.
—WILLIAM SHAKESPEARE

*W*isdom is ofttimes nearer when we stoop
Than when we soar.

— WILLIAM WORDSWORTH

*W*isdom denotes the pursuing of the best ends
by the best means.

— FRANCES HUTCHESON

*T*he wise man forgets insults as the ungrateful
forget benefits.

— CHINESE PROVERB

*T*he clouds may drop down titles and estates;
Wealth may seek us; but wisdom must be sought.
———EDWARD YOUNG

*H*e who has imagination without learning has
wings but no feet.
———FRENCH PROVERB

*O*ur wisest reflections (if the word wise may be
given to humanity) are tainted by our hopes
and fears.
———MARY WORTLEY MONTAGU

*I*t requires wisdom to understand wisdom; the music is nothing if the audience is deaf.
—WALTER LIPPMANN

A wise man, to accomplish his end, may even carry his foe on his shoulder.
—PANCHATANTRA

*W*isdom is divided into two parts: (a) having a great deal to say, and (b) not saying it.
—ANONYMOUS

Those who wish to appear wise among fools,
among the wise seem foolish.
———Quintillian

There are two sentences inscribed upon the
Delphic oracle . . . : "Know thyself" and
"Nothing too much"; and upon these all
other precepts depend.
———Plutarch

Common sense in an uncommon degree is what
the world calls wisdom.
———Anonymous

To know one's self is wisdom, but to know one's
neighbor is genius.
—ANNA ANDRIM

A man's wisdom is most conspicuous where he is
able to distinguish among dangers and make
choice of the least.
—MACHIAVELLI

Knowledge is proud that he has learned so
much;
Wisdom is humble that he knows no more.
—WILLIAM COWPER

*K*nowledge can be communicated, but not
wisdom. One can find it, live it, be fortified
by it, do wonders through it, but one cannot
communicate and teach it.
—HERMANN HESSE

*M*oney does not prevent you from becoming
lame.
You may be ill in any part of your body,
So it is better for you to go and think again
And to select wisdom.
—IFA YORUBAN

Old places and old persons in their turn, when spirit dwells in them, have an intrinsic vitality of which youth is incapable; precisely the balance and wisdom that comes from long perspectives and broad foundations.

—GEORGE SANTAYANA

Common sense is not so common.

—VOLTAIRE

Wonder is the beginning of wisdom.

—GREEK PROVERB

The art of being wise is the art of knowing what
to overlook.
—WILLIAM JAMES

The eyes are of little use if the mind be blind.
—ARAB PROVERB

Knowledge alone is not enough. It must be
leavened with magnanimity before it becomes
wisdom.
—ADLAI E. STEVENSON

*A*ll wisdom comes from the Lord,
And remains with him forever.
The sand of the seas, and the drops of rain,
And the days of eternity—who can count them?
The height of the heavens, and the breadth of the
     earth,
And the deep, and wisdom—who can track them
     out?
Wisdom was created before them all,
And sound intelligence from eternity.

—BEN SIRA

*N*ot to know is bad, but not to wish to know is worse.

—WEST AFRICAN PROVERB

*T*o know how to grow old is the master-work of wisdom, and one of the most difficult chapters in the great art of living.

—HENRI FRÉDÉRIC AMIEL

*T*he function of wisdom is to discriminate between good and evil.

—CICERO

*T*he doorstep to the temple of wisdom is a
knowledge of our own ignorance.
—CHARLES H. SPURGEON

A questioning man is halfway to being wise.
—IRISH PROVERB

*I*f one is too lazy to think, too vain to do a thing
badly, too cowardly to admit it, one will never
attain wisdom.
—CYRIL CONNOLLY

*S*o teach us to number our days, that we may
apply our hearts unto wisdom.

—PSALM 90:12

*I*f there were wisdom in beards, all goats would
be prophets.

—ARMENIAN PROVERB

*W*hen you have got an elephant by the hind legs
and he is trying to run away, it's best to let
him run.

—ABRAHAM LINCOLN

*P*ain makes man think. Thought makes man wise. Wisdom makes life endurable.

— JOHN PATRICK

*G*reat wisdom consists in not demanding too much of human nature, and yet not altogether spoiling it by indulgence.

— LIN YUTANG

*H*e is a wise man who does not grieve for the things which he has not, but rejoices for those which he has.

— EPICTETUS

*I*n seeking wisdom, thou art wise; in imagining
that thou hast attained it, thou art a fool.
—BEN SIRA

*I*t is unwise to be too sure of one's own wisdom. It
is healthy to be reminded that the strongest
might weaken and the wisest might err.
—MAHATMA GANDHI

*W*isdom is knowing what to do next;
Skill is knowing how to do it, and Virtue is doing it.
—DAVID STARR JORDAN

A man cannot leave his wisdom or his experience to his heirs.

———ITALIAN PROVERB

*M*any persons might have attained to wisdom had they not assumed that they already possessed it.

———SENECA

*W*isdom is an affair of values, and of value judgments. It is intelligent conduct of human affairs.

———SYDNEY HOOK

*S*even characteristics distinguish the wise: he does
  not speak in the presence of one wiser than
  himself, does not interrupt, is not hasty to
  answer, asks and answers the point, talks about
  first things first and about last things last,
  admits when he does not know, and acknowl-
  edges the truth.

  —TALMUD

*T*he man who views the world at fifty the same
  as he did at twenty has wasted thirty years of
  his life.

  —MUHAMMAD ALI

A wise man hears one word and understands two.
—JEWISH PROVERB

*A*t twenty-two, I thought I knew everything. Now, at sixty-seven, I find I haven't tasted a drop from the sea of knowledge. The more I learn, the more I find out how little I know.
—JOHN COPAGE

A man doesn't begin to attain wisdom until he recognizes that he is no longer indispensable.
—ADMIRAL BYRD

*T*o wisdom belongs the intellectual apprehension of eternal things; to knowledge, the rational knowledge of temporal things.

—SAINT AUGUSTINE

*I*t may be a mistake to mix different wines, but old and new wisdom mix admirably.

—BERTOLT BRECHT

*W*isdom is ever a blessing; education is sometimes a curse.

—JOHN A. SHEDD

The road to wisdom? Well, it's plain
And simple to express;
Err
And err
And err again
But less
And less
And less.
—PIET HEIN

The first dawn of smartness is to stop trying things
you don't know anything about—especially if
they run to anything over a dollar.
—WILSON MIZNER

*N*ot to know certain things is a great part of wisdom.
—HUGO GROTIUS

*A*lmost every wise saying has an opposite one, no less wise, to balance it.
—GEORGE SANTAYANA

*I*t's taken me all my life to understand that it is not necessary to understand everything.
—RENÉ COTY

*H*e is no wise man that cannot play the fool
upon occasion.
—THOMAS FULLER, M.D.

*W*hat a man knows at fifty that he did not know
at twenty is for the most part incommunicable.
—ADLAI E. STEVENSON

*N*ine-tenths of wisdom consists in being wise
in time.
—THEODORE ROOSEVELT

To have lived long does not necessarily imply the
gathering of much wisdom and experience.
A man who has pedaled twenty-five thousand
miles on a stationary bicycle has not circled the
globe. He has only garnered weariness.
—PAUL ELDRIDGE

To know when to be generous and when firm—
this is wisdom.
—ELBERT HUBBARD

No man is born wise.
—CERVANTES

*T*he seat of knowledge is in the head; of wisdom, in the heart. We are sure to judge wrong if we do not feel right.

—WILLIAM HAZLITT

*G*reat is wisdom; infinite is the value of wisdom. It cannot be exaggerated; it is the highest achievement of man.

—THOMAS CARLYLE

*N*o man was ever wise by chance.

—SENECA

A person who doesn't know but knows that he
doesn't know is a student; teach him. A person
who knows but who doesn't know that he
knows is asleep; awaken him. But a person
who knows and knows that he knows is wise;
follow him.

— ASIAN PROVERB

*T*o my extreme mortification, I grow wiser
every day.

— MARY WORTLEY MONTAGU

*W*isdom cries out in the streets and no man regards it.

——WILLIAM SHAKESPEARE

*W*ise men are not wise all the time.

——RALPH WALDO EMERSON

A man should never be ashamed to own he has been in the wrong, which is but saying, in other words, that he is wiser today than he was yesterday.

——JONATHAN SWIFT

*T*he height of heaven, the breadth of the earth, the
abyss, and wisdom—who can search them out?
—APOCRYPHA, ECCLESIASTICUS

*W*ise people learn not to dread but actually to
welcome problems because it is in this whole
process of meeting and solving problems that
life has its meaning.
—M. SCOTT PECK, M.D.

*W*e can be wise from goodness and good from
wisdom.
—MARIE VON EBNER-ESCHENBACK

The price of wisdom is above rubies.
———Job 28:18

There is this difference between happiness and
    wisdom: He that thinks himself the happiest
    man, really is so; but he that thinks himself the
    wisest, is generally the greatest fool.
———Charles Caleb Colton

He is not wise who is not wise for himself.
———English proverb

The mouth of a wise man is in his heart.
—BENJAMIN FRANKLIN

The true sage is not he who sees, but he who,
seeing the furthest, has the deepest love for
mankind.
—MAURICE MAETERLINCK

It is the province of knowledge to speak and it is
the privilege of wisdom to listen.
—OLIVER WENDELL HOLMES SR.

*C*ommon sense suits itself to the ways of the world. Wisdom tries to conform to the ways of Heaven.
—JOSEPH JOUBERT

*I*t is very foolish to wish to be exclusively wise.
—LA ROCHEFOUCAULD

*T*o say witty things is not always a sign of wisdom.
—GREEK PROVERB

*W*isdom is always an overmatch for strength.

—PHAEDRUS

*N*ot by years but by disposition is wisdom
   acquired.

—PLAUTUS

*Y*ou, seeker after knowledge,
look for the Oneness within.

—HADEWIJCH OF ANTWERP

*W*isdom had rather be buffeted than not listened to.

———Publilius Syrus

*T*hose who seek the truth by means of intellect and learning only get further and further away from it. Not till your thoughts cease all their branching here and there, not till you abandon all thoughts of seeking for something, not till your mind is motionless as wood or stone will you be on the right road to the Gate.

———Huang Po

*N*ot by constraint or severity shall you have access to true wisdom, but by abandonment, and childlike mirthfulness. If you would know aught, be gay before it.

——HENRY DAVID THOREAU

*W*e have two ears, but only one mouth, so that we may listen more and talk less.

——ZENO OF ELEA

*S*ciences may be learned by rote, but wisdom not.

——LAURENCE STERNE

*W*e know accurately only when we know little;
with knowledge doubt increases.
—JOHANN WOLFGANG VON GOETHE

*L*osing an illusion makes you wiser than finding
a truth.
—LUDWIG BÖRNE

*I*t takes a wise man to recognize a wise man.
—XENOPHANES

$\mathcal{I}$t is not the answer that enlightens, but the question.

—EUGÈNE IONESCO

$\mathcal{W}$isdom is not an art that may be learned; wisdom comes from the stars.

—PAUL FLEMMING

$\mathcal{W}$ise men talk because they have something to say; fools talk because they have to say something.

—PLATO

It is better to keep one's mouth shut and be thought a fool than to open it and resolve all doubt.

—ABRAHAM LINCOLN

Wisdom is a spirit devoted to man's good.

—APOCRYPHA, WISDOM OF SOLOMON

Wisdom does not live in only one house.

—ASHANTI PROVERB

What is impenetrable to us really exists, manifesting itself as the highest wisdom and the most radiant beauty.

—ALBERT EINSTEIN

But he who seeks the flowers of truth,
Must quit the garden for the field.

—GEORGE GORDON, LORD BYRON

Wisdom is stronger than fate.

—LATIN PROVERB

*W*isdom too often never comes, and so one ought
not to reject it merely because it comes late.
—FELIX FRANKFURTER

*I*t is by logic that we prove, but by intuition that
we discover.
—HENRI POINCARÉ

A fool sees not the same tree that a wise man
sees.
—WILLIAM BLAKE

The more I read, the more I meditate; and the more I acquire, the more certain I am that I know nothing.

—Voltaire

We don't understand life any better at forty than at twenty, but by then we realize and admit it.

—Jules Renard

The only medicine for suffering, crime, and all the other woes of mankind, is wisdom.

—T. H. Huxley

*H*e dares to be a fool, and that is the first step in the direction of wisdom.
—JAMES G. HUNEKER

*W*isdom lies not in reason, but in love.
—ANDRÉ GIDE

*W*e do not receive wisdom, we have to discover it for ourselves by a voyage that no one can take for us.
—MARCEL PROUST

I said, "I will be wise," but it was far from me.
—ECCLESIASTES 7:23

*T*he next year, the next decade, in all likelihood the next generation, will require more bravery and wisdom on our part than any period in our history. We will be face to face, every day, in every part of our lives and times, with the real issue of our age—the issue of survival.
—JOHN F. KENNEDY

The divine essence itself is love and wisdom.
—EMANUEL SWEDENBORG

Wisdom is not finally tested in the schools,
Wisdom cannot be pass'd from one having it to
another not having it,
Wisdom is of the soul. . . .
—WALT WHITMAN

The more accurately we search into the human
mind, the stronger traces we everywhere find
of the wisdom of Him who made it.
—EDMUND BURKE

A wise companion is half the journey.
——RUSSIAN PROVERB

A wise man has no extensive knowledge.
He who has extensive knowledge is not a wise man.
The sage does not accumulate for himself.
The more he gives to others, the more he possesses
   of his own.
——LAO-TZU

*W*isdom is not wisdom when it is derived from
   books alone.
——HORACE

*P*eople are never so near playing the fool as
when they think themselves wise.
—MARY WORTLEY MONTAGU

A wise man's question contains half the answer.
—SOLOMON IBN GABIROL

*I*t's bad taste to be wise all the time, like being at a
perpetual funeral.
—D. H. LAWRENCE

*W*isdom is only a comparative quality, it will not bear a single definition.

— MARQUESS OF HALIFAX

*I*t is not enough to have a good mind. The main thing is to use it well.

— RENÉ DESCARTES

A man is not necessarily intelligent because he has plenty of ideas, any more than he is a good general because he has plenty of soldiers.

— CHAMFORT

*R*eason's last step is the recognition that there are an infinite number of things which are beyond it.

— PASCAL

I called for help, and there came to me a spirit of wisdom. I valued her above scepter and throne, and reckoned riches as nothing beside her; I counted no precious stone her equal, because all the gold in the world compared with her is but a little sand, and silver worth no more than clay.

— APOCRYPHA, WISDOM OF SOLOMON

*S*eeing through is rarely seeing into.
— ELIZABETH BIBESCO

*A*ll this wordly wisdom was once the unamiable heresy of some wise man.
— HENRY DAVID THOREAU

*W*ho is wise? He who learns from all men, as it is said. From all my teachers have I gotten understanding.
— BEN ZOMA

*S*ome folks are wise, and some are otherwise.
—TOBIAS SMOLLETT

*W*isdom giveth life to them that have it.
—ECCLESIASTES 7:12

*W*isdom makes a weak man strong, a poor man king, a good generation of a bad one, and a foolish man reasonable.
—IRISH PROVERB

*H*istory teaches us that men and nations behave wisely once they have exhausted all other alternatives.

—ABBA EBAN

*W*e should be careful to get out of an experience only the wisdom that is in it—and stop there, lest we be like the cat that sits down on a hot stove lid. She will never sit on a hot stove lid again—and that is well; but also she will never sit down on a cold one anymore.

—MARK TWAIN

The hardest thing to learn in life is which bridge
to cross and which to burn.
—David L. Russell

We pay a high price for being intelligent.
Wisdom hurts.
—Euripides

It is better to know some of the questions than to
know all the answers.
—James Thurber

*W*e do not know one-millionth of one percent about anything.

—THOMAS A. EDISON

*G*ood people are good because they've come to wisdom through failure. We get very little wisdom from success, you know.

—WILLIAM SAROYAN

*M*an can learn nothing except by going from the known to the unknown.

—CLAUDE BERNARD

*I*t's what you learn after you know it all that
counts.
— WOODEN

*W*e're drowning in information and starving for
knowledge.
— RUTHERFORD D. ROGERS

*F*ools get things mixed up and wise men
straighten them out.
— SCOTTISH PROVERB

*B*efore God we are all equally wise and equally foolish.

—ALBERT EINSTEIN

*W*isdom is the reward you get for a lifetime of listening when you'd have preferred to talk.

—DOUG LARSON

I am learning all the time. The tombstone will be my diploma.

—EARTHA KITT

*K*nowledge and wisdom, far from being one,
    Have ofttimes no connection. Knowledge
      dwells
In heads replete with thoughts of other men;
Wisdom in minds attentive to their own.
         —WILLIAM COWPER

*S*ince we cannot know all that is to be known of
    everything, we ought to know a little about
    everything.
         —BLAISE PASCAL

*N*ever mistake knowledge for wisdom. One helps you make a living; the other helps you make a life.

— SANDRA CAREY

*W*isdom consists of the anticipation of consequences.

— NORMAN COUSINS

*W*isdom is the quality that keeps you from getting into situations where you need it.

— DOUG LARSON

It is only with the heart that one can see rightly;
what is essential is invisible to the eye.
—ANTOINE DE SAINT-EXUPÉRY

Wisdom is never dear, provided the article be
genuine.
—HORACE GREELEY

People far prefer happiness to wisdom, but this
is like wanting to be immortal without getting
older.
—SYDNEY J. HARRIS

*L*earning sleeps and snores in libraries, but
wisdom is everywhere, wide awake, on tiptoe.
—JOSH BILLINGS

*T*he most powerful weapon on earth is the human
soul on fire.
—FERDINAND FOCH

*T*he test of a first-rate intelligence is the ability
to hold two opposed ideas in the mind at
the same time, and still retain the ability to
function.
—F. SCOTT FITZGERALD

He who knows others is learned; he who knows himself is wise.

—LAO-TZU

The little I know, I owe to my ignorance.

—SACHA GUITRY

Man's mind stretched to a new idea never goes back to its original dimensions.

—OLIVER WENDELL HOLMES SR.

*T*here often seems to be a playfulness to wise
people, as if either their equanimity has as its
source this playfulness or the playfulness flows
from the equanimity; and they can persuade
other people who are in a state of agitation to
calm down and manage a smile.

—EDWARD HOAGLAND

*D*efer not till to-morrow to be wise,
To-morrow's sun to thee may never rise.

—CONGREVE

*I*f a man empties his purse into his head, no one can take it from him.
———BENJAMIN FRANKLIN

*T*o be a philosopher is not merely to have subtle thoughts, nor even to found a school, but so to love wisdom as to live, according to its dictates, a life of simplicity, independence, magnanimity, and trust.
———HENRY DAVID THOREAU

*T*he wisdom of life consists in the elimination of nonessentials.
— LIN YUTANG

*T*he first key to wisdom is this—constant and frequent questioning . . . for by doubting we are led to question and by questioning we arrive at the truth.
— PETER ABELARD

*M*en are wise in proportion not to their experience but to their capacity for experience.
— GEORGE BERNARD SHAW

*T*he life of wisdom must be a life of contemplation combined with action.

— M. Scott Peck, M.D.

*A*pplicants for wisdom, do what I have done: Inquire within.

— Heraclitus

*S*elf-reflection is the school of wisdom.

— Baltasar Gracián y Morales

The most important wisdom I can offer is to never let others define your horizons. Identify what success means to you and then keep your eye on that prize.

—KAY KOPLOVITZ

Only in the oasis of silence can we drink deeply from our inner cup of wisdom.

—SUE PATTON THOELE

The older I grow the more I distrust the familiar doctrine that age brings wisdom.

—H. L. MENCKEN

*W*ise men learn more from fools than fools from wise men.

—CATO

*B*y the time your life is finished, you will have learned just enough to begin it well.

—ELEANOR MARX

*H*e whose wisdom cannot help him, gets no good from being wise.

—ENNIUS

Though a man be wise,
It is no shame for him to live and learn.
———Sophocles

Be wise with speed;
A fool at forty is a fool indeed.
———Edward Young

Walls crumble, and we get to the essence of
who we are.
———Christiane Northrup, M.D.

*K*nowledge without wisdom is a load of books
on the back of an ass.
—JAPANESE PROVERB

*S*ee the inevitable changes not as threats but
as opportunities that can deepen our understanding and bring us wisdom and growth.
—SUSAN L. TAYLOR

*T*he conventional wisdom is always the obverse of
what actually happens. You have to look back-
ward to see ahead.
—ROGER CASS

*W*isdom comes with age, but keep it to yourself. Sentences that begin "I don't want to tell you what to do with your life, but . . ." should stop right there.

———MARY ROACH

*A*s light is pleasant to the eye, so is truth to the understanding.

———RICHARD PELHAM

*W*hen wisdom becomes conventional, it's time to ask questions.

———BETHANY MCLEAN

*I*n seeking Wisdom, the first state is silence, the
    second listening, the third remembrance, the
    fourth practicing, the fifth teaching.
        —RABBI SOLOMON IBN GABIROL

*E*ducation is much more than learning a body of
    knowledge. It is living wisdom.
        —ANNE WILSON SCHAEF

*T*o attain knowledge, add things every day. To
    attain wisdom, remove things every day.
        —LAO-TZU

*T*o walk safely through the maze of human life,
one needs the light of wisdom and the guid-
ance of virtue.

—BUDDHA

*W*isdom is knowing when you can't be wise.

—MUHAMMAD ALI

A man begins cutting his wisdom teeth the first
time he bites off more than he can chew.

—IRISH SAYING

To know how to grow old is the master work of
  wisdom.
                    —HENRI FREDERIC AMIEL

The ultimate truth, wisdom, and mystery of the
  Universe is far deeper, higher, wider, and
  richer than any name or image we use to
  refer to it.
                    —PATRICIA LYNN REILLY

Trust the wisdom of your body, for it often reflects
  the wisdom of your soul.
                    —MELODY BEATTIE

*W*isdom doesn't necessarily come with age. Sometimes age just shows up all by itself.
—TOM WILSON

*E*very single ancient wisdom and religion will tell you the same thing—don't live entirely for yourself, live for other people. Don't get stuck inside your own ego, because it will become a prison in no time flat.
—BARBARA WARD

A word to the wise is infuriating.
—ANONYMOUS

*I*f you realize you aren't so wise today as you
thought you were yesterday, you're wiser today.
—OLIN MILLER

*T*here are two things to aim at in life: first to get
what you want and, after that, to enjoy it. Only
the wisest of mankind achieve the second.
—LOGAN PEARSALL SMITH

*I*t is easier to get older than wiser.
—BARBARA JOHNSON

The wisdom of age isn't limited to people of
   advanced years.
   —QUINN ELI

The wise person speaks carefully and with truth,
   for every word that passes through one's teeth
   is meant for something.
   —MOLEFI KETE ASIANTE

The good Lord set definite limits on man's
   wisdom, but set no limits on his stupidity—
   and that's just not fair!
   —KONRAD ADENAUER

The quieter you become, the more you can hear.
——Baba Ram Dass

When our knowledge coalesces with our humanity and our humor, it can add up to wisdom.
——Carol Orlock

That which seems the height of absurdity in one generation often becomes the height of wisdom in the next.
——John Stuart Mill

*I*t wasn't raining when Noah built the ark.
—HOWARD RUFF

A wise man gets more use from his enemies than
a fool from his friends.
—BALTASAR GRACIÁN Y MORALES

*T*he foolish person seeks happiness in the distance;
the wise person grows it under his feet.
—JAMES OPPENHEIM

I prefer the errors of enthusiasm to the
indifference of wisdom.
———ANATOLE FRANCE

*T*he steadfastness of the wise is but the art of
keeping their agitation locked in their hearts.
———LA ROCHEFOUCAULD

*Y*ou look wise. Pray correct that error.
———CHARLES LAMB

*S*ubtlety is not a proof of wisdom.

—PUSHKIN

*G*od Almighty never created a man half as wise
as he looks.

—THOMAS CARLYLE

*T*omorrow a stranger will say with masterly good
sense precisely what we have thought and felt
all the time.

—RALPH WALDO EMERSON

*A*n optimist is a person who sees a green light everywhere. The pessimist sees only the red light. But the truly wise person is color blind.

—ALBERT SCHWEITZER

*W*isdom is the right use of knowledge. To know is not to be wise. Many men know a great deal, and are all the greater fools for it. There is no fool so great as a knowing fool. But to know how to use knowledge is to have wisdom.

—CHARLES H. SPURGEON

*I*n the deep, unwritten wisdom of life there are
many things to be learned that cannot be
taught. We never know them by hearing them
spoken, but we grow into them by experience
and recognize them through understanding.
—ANTHONY HOPE

*T*he price of wisdom is eternal thought.
—FRANK BIRCH

*T*hrough wisdom a house is built and through
understanding it is established.
—PROVERBS 24:3

There is no purifier in this world equal to wisdom.
—BHAGAVAD GITA

Deliberate often—decide once.
—LATIN PROVERB

Wisdom does not show itself so much in precept
as in life—in firmness of mind and a mastery
of appetite. It teaches us to do as well as to talk,
and to make our words and actions all of a
color.
—SENECA

*W*isdom outweighs any wealth.
— SOPHOCLES

A proverb is one man's wit and all men's wisdom.
— JOHN RUSSELL

*M*en who know themselves are no longer fools; they stand on the threshold of the Door of Wisdom.
— HAVELOCK ELLIS

*T*he wise have a solid sense of silence and the
ability to keep a storehouse of secrets. Their
capacity and character are respected.
—BALTASAR GRACIÁN Y MORALES

*T*he eye sees only what the mind is prepared to
comprehend.
—HENRI BERGSON

*T*he universe is full of magical things, patiently
waiting for our wits to grow sharper.
—EDEN PHILLIPOTTS

*W*isdom is perishable. Unlike information or knowledge, it cannot be stored in a computer or recorded in a book. It expires with each passing generation.

—SID TAYLOR

*W*isdom and goodness are twin-born, one heart
Must hold both sisters, never seen apart.

—WILLIAM COWPER

*H*e that has grown to wisdom hurries not,
But thinks and weighs what wisdom bids him do.

—GUIDO GUINICELLI

There is often wisdom under a shabby cloak.
———Caecilius Statius

For when I dinna clearly see,
I always own I dinna ken,
And that's the way with wisest men.
———Allan Ramsay

Be wiser than other people if you can; but do not
tell them so.
———Lord Chesterfield

*I*t is not wisdom to be only wise,
And on the inward vision close the eyes,
But it is wisdom to believe the heart.
———George Santayana

*O*ne should take good care not to grow too wise
for so great a pleasure of life as laughter.
———Joseph Addison

*W*isdom begins at the end.
———Daniel Webster

*A*n intelligent man knows all the right answers;
a wise man knows all the right questions.
—JOHN DIELSI

A wise old owl sat in an oak,
The more he saw the less he spoke,
The less he spoke the more he heard,
Why can't we all be like that wise old bird?
—ANONYMOUS

A wise man turns chance into good fortune.
—THOMAS FULLER, M.D.

Too many wish to be happy before becoming wise.
—SUSANNE CURCHOD NECKER

Of what use is wisdom when the butter won't stick to the bread?
—DUTCH PROVERB

He that breaks a thing to find out what it is has left the path of wisdom.
—J.R.R. TOLKIEN

There is little room left for wisdom when one is
full of judgment.
—MALCOLM HEIN

Mistakes are the usual bridge between inexperi-
ence and wisdom.
—PHYLLIS THEROUX

To acquire knowledge, one must study; but to
acquire wisdom, one must observe.
—MARILYN VOS SAVANT

*W*isdom is knowing when to speak your mind and when to mind your speech.

—EVANGEL

*W*isdom is like electricity. There is no permanently wise man, but men capable of wisdom, who, being put into certain company, or other favorable conditions, become wise for a short time, as glasses rubbed acquire electric power for a while.

—RALPH WALDO EMERSON

The doors of wisdom are never shut.

—FRANKLIN

The man who questions opinions is wise. The man who quarrels with facts is a fool.

—FRANK GARBUTT

They would need to be already wise, in order to love wisdom.

—JOHANN FRIEDRICH VON SCHILLER

*W*isdom is the power to put our time and our knowledge to the proper use.
— THOMAS J. WATSON

A little nonsense now and then is relished by the wisest men.
— ROALD DAHL

A prudent question is one half of wisdom.
— FRANCIS BACON

*S*cience is organized knowledge. Wisdom is organized life.
—IMMANUEL KANT

*T*he invariable mark of wisdom is to see the miraculous in the common.
—RALPH WALDO EMERSON

*T*he fool wanders, a wise man travels.
—THOMAS FULLER

*O*ne's first step in wisdom is to question everything—and one's last is to come to terms with everything.

—GEORG CHRISTOPH LICHTENBERG

*I*t is not white hair that engenders wisdom.

—MENANDER

*H*e bids fair to grow wise who has discovered that he is not so.

—PUBLILIUS SYRUS

*N*ot to engage in the pursuit of ideas is to live like ants instead of men.
—MORTIMER ADLER

*K*nowledge speaks, but wisdom listens.
—JIMI HENDRIX

*T*he more sand that has escaped from the hourglass of our life, the clearer we should see through it.
—JEAN PAUL

*D*o not seek to follow in the footsteps of the wise.
Seek what they sought.
———BASHO

A man may learn wisdom even from a foe.
———ARISTOPHANES

I believe that all wisdom consists in caring
immensely for a few right things, and not
caring a straw about the rest.
———SIR JOHN BUCHAN

Intelligence is when you spot a flaw in your boss's reasoning. Wisdom is when you refrain from pointing it out.
—JAMES DENT

Without courage, wisdom bears no fruit.
—BALTASAR GRACIÁN Y MORALES

The beginning of wisdom is calling things by their right names.
—CHINESE PROVERB

*I*t is the mark of an educated mind to be able to entertain a thought without accepting it.
———ARISTOTLE

*W*isdom comes by disillusionment.
———GEORGE SANTAYANA

*T*hrough what is near, one understands what is far away.
———HSUN-TZU

The real voyage of discovery consists not in seeking new landscapes, but in having new eyes.
— MARCEL PROUST

If wisdom were offered me with this restriction, that I should keep it close and not communicate it, I would refuse the gift.
— SENECA

The important thing is not to stop questioning.
— ALBERT EINSTEIN

*W*e learn wisdom from failure much more than from success. We often discover what will do, by finding out what will not do; and probably he who never made a mistake never made a discovery.

—SAMUEL SMILES

*S*eek the wisdom of the ages, but look at the world through the eyes of a child.

—RON WILD

*L*et my heart be wise. It is the gods' best gift.

—EURIPIDES

*D*are to be wise.
—HORACE

*S*elf-examination is the key to insight, which is
the key to wisdom.
—M. SCOTT PECK, M.D.

*I*nsight doesn't happen often on the click of the
moment, like a lucky snapshot, but comes in its
own time and more slowly and from nowhere
but within.
—EUDORA WELTY

*I*n what we really understand, we reason but
  little.
  —WILLIAM HAZLITT

*W*hen we stay close to the wisdom of our own
  knowing, seeking solutions to our problems in
  the sanctuary of the heart and not in the vanity
  of the mind, then we can pretty much trust in
  the unfolding, mysterious wisdom of life.
  —MARIANNE WILLIAMSON

*T*hinking is the soul talking to itself.
  —PLATO

*A*ll the glory of greatness has not luster for
    people who are in search of understanding.
                        —PASCAL

*T*he wisest man is he who does not fancy that he is
    so at all.
                        —NICOLAS BOILEAU

*W*isdom is the principal thing; therefore get
    wisdom; and with all thy getting get
    understanding.
                        —PROVERBS 4:7

The wave is ignorant of the true nature of the
    sea: How can the temporal comprehend
    the eternal?
                —SA'IB OF TABRIZ

And Wisdom cries, "I know not anything";
And only Faith beholds that all is well.
                —SIDNEY LYSAGHT

Knowledge, when wisdom is too weak to guide
    her,
Is like a headstrong horse, that throws the rider.
                —FRANCIS QUARLES

[125]

*M*ake wisdom your provision for the journey from youth to old age, for it is a more certain support than all other possessions.

———BIAS

*W*isdom is easy to carry but difficult to gather.

———CZECH PROVERB

*T*he growth of understanding follows an ascending spiral rather than a straight line.

———JOANNA FIELD

THE TEXT OF THIS BOOK IS SET IN GRANJON
BY MSPACE, KATONAH, NEW YORK.

BOOK DESIGN BY MAURA FADDEN ROSENTHAL